90 Days to Write Your Way to Spring

The Winter Journal

Wade Forbes

90 Days to Write Your Way to Spring

The Winter Journal

Wade Forbes

Print: 978-1-944027-90-2

www.networlding.com

Layout and Design by Trembling Giant Marketing, LLC.
www.TremblingGiantMarketing.com

This book is dedicated to my beautiful wife Megan and sons Owen and Ryan. Thank you for inspiring me to make these quotes everyday during COVID-19 and this journal possible.

Introduction.

In 2017, I began drawing quotes. I drew quotes for my children to read every day at lunch to discuss with their friends. I drew quotes for strangers in bars and restaurants while I traveled for work. I drew a quote for the man who sold me my used car to help inspire him to land his dream job one day. And then, in a moment that is still so fleeting, I started drawing quotes for people who were doing the best they could in a little coffee shop in Maryland, but not getting the kindness they deserved.

This moment began a journey for me that lasted 11 months, spreading my own brand of kindness and hope by illustrating quotes for a group of wonderful people. Then COVID-19 shifted our world and shut down my work and the coffee shop in March of 2020.

At first, I found myself sitting in my house imagining all the ways things could go wrong, but then I began drawing quotes to calm my nerves, fill myself with hope, and remain positive when the world just had to wait and see what would happen. My ritual of drawing one quote each day continued as I counted the days and weeks to help me, and I began to share them on social media platforms. With each day I noticed more and more people telling me about how these illustrations and the quotes they focused on made them feel, and often helping them imagine all the ways things could go right.

Through this experience it has become clear to me that we must create a practice, a little each day, to believe that things are going to be ok. Not just ok in the sense of food, shelter, and safety, but truly believing that we are going to show up for one another in a way that makes the world we want; the world we believe we can have. This is what this journal is to me, and I hope it will be the same for you - for you to make it what you need to grow through whatever you are going through. Let's jump right in...

It has been said that you won't know when you'll stumble onto something great. You wake up one day, and head out the door to experience something that changes the trajectory of your life, of someone else's life and even many lives there after.

Those pivotal moments seem to come down to two things: did you do it or did you wait for someone else to do it? Did you take the chance to do something and create change, or wait to see what happens?

What if we could bottle up the feeling we get when we do something nice, and then return to that feeling when we need it? Life sure would feel a lot easier. The reality is that many times we get overrun by the difficulty, the struggle, or the challenges we face and we hesitate to act - and those pivotal moments fade away.

Choosing to act is like building muscle memory - pay attention to your form, remain consistent, demonstrate healthy behaviors if you want to improve, and be sure to keep track of the steps you took so others can join in.

What if we could start something and continue it for as long as it takes? Create a movement that was worth spreading that no one could argue with? Stop telling stories about someone else's kindness and make ourselves one of the main characters? It's time to put in the work.

A bit of advice: as you begin your quote journal journey, be prepared to learn some things about yourself you didn't know you were capable of. Start to imagine what changes will take place when you commit to reflecting once a day. See what is possible when you drown out the noise and show up for yourself in a way that leads to something amazing. Leave the doubts and troubles of your past aside for now.

How This Journal Is Meant To Be Used.

Throw your ideas and desires onto the pages to help your reality take shape. Underneath each illustration is a space for you to doodle, dream, draw. Begin to imagine that, at the end, you won't be the same person you were when you started. Show kindness to yourself, and see what happens. You may even notice mistakes in the drawings in this journal which I left on purpose because no one is perfect. At the end of this journal, take a moment to reflect on what you've learned over the last 90 days and what you'd like to take with you into Spring.

What do the numbers on the quotes mean? This daily practice helped me reflect throughout the pandemic and those are references to me originally counting the days, but in this journal, they are not in any particular order.

BE YOURSELF;
EVERYONE ELSE IS
ALREADY
TAKEN.
-Oscar
Wilde

"THERE ARE NO
BEAUTIFUL
SURFACES
WITHOUT A
TERRIBLE
DEPTH."
–Friedrich
Nietzsche
W.F.
'20

"LEADERSHIP
HAS NO RANK."
—NJK

EXPERIENCE
IS SIMPLY THE
NAME WE GIVE
OUR MISTAKES.
—Oscar Wilde
W.F. 20

I HAVE FOUND THAT THE PROCESS OF DISCOVERING WHO I REALLY AM BEGINS WITH KNOWING WHO I REALLY DON'T WANT TO BE.
-Anonymous
WF.20

"HANG IN THERE.
(deep breath)
IT IS ASTONISHING
HOW SHORT A TIME
IT CAN TAKE FOR
VERY WONDERFUL
THINGS TO HAPPEN."
-Frances Eliza Hodgson
WF.20

"THOSE WHO ARE THE HAPPIEST ARE THOSE WHO DO THE MOST FOR OTHERS."
-Booker T. Washington

"THE ONLY PERSON YOU ARE DESTINED TO BECOME IS THE PERSON YOU DECIDE TO BE."
–Ralph Waldo Emerson
WF. 20

FAITH
DOESN'T MAKE
SENSE. IT
MAKES MIRACLES.
-Psalm 77:14
WF '20

"TELL ME AND
I FORGET.
TEACH ME AND
I REMEMBER.
INVOLVE ME
AND I LEARN."

-Benjamin Franklin

A LIE MAY TAKE CARE OF
THE PRESENT, BUT IT
HAS NO FUTURE.
–Anonymous

"AUTUMN SHOWS US HOW BEAUTIFUL IT IS TO LET THINGS GO."
– Unknown
WF '20
DAY 203

MY PROBLEMS
FADE TO
THE
BACKGROUND
AS I
REACH
OUT TO OTHERS."
-Unknown
DAY 210
@wadeforbes

"the greatest pleasure in life is doing what people say you cannot do."
WF '20

NEVER WATER YOURSELF
DOWN JUST BECAUSE
SOMEONE CAN'T HANDLE
YOU AT 100 PROOF.
—Unknown
DAY 192
WF'20

W.F. '20
THERE'S JUST ONE LEGITIMATE
SYNONYM FOR FRIDAY:
boom shakalaka

"A FRIEND IS ONE WHO OVERLOOKS YOUR BROKEN FENCE AND ADMIRES THE FLOWERS IN YOUR GARDEN."
—Unknown

"SOME PEOPLE GRUMBLE THAT ROSES HAVE THORNS. I AM GRATEFUL THAT THORNS HAVE ROSES."
-Alphonse Karr
WF20

WHEN A KING HAS GOOD COUNSELORS,
HIS REIGN IS PEACEFUL.
-African Proverb
WF '20

WE CANNOT SEE
OUR REFLECTION
IN RUNNING
WATER, IT IS
ONLY IN STILL
WATER THAT
WE CAN SEE.
–Zen proverb

"A seed grows with no sound, but a tree falls with huge noise. Destruction has noise, but creation is quiet. This is the power of silence

GROW SILENTLY."

—Unknown

"YOU WEREN'T BORN TO JUST PAY BILLS
AND DIE."
—Unknown

WF. 20
"MAY TODAY BE THE
FRIDAYEST FRIDAY THAT
EVER FRIDAYED."
Anonymous

" BE
HAPPY
LIVING
FOR YOU
ARE A
LONG
TIME
DEAD."
-Scottish
Proverb
WF.20

날개
말
"WORDS HAVE NO WINGS BUT CAN FLY A THOUSAND MILES."
-Korean Proverb
WF.'20

"DON'T LOSE HOPE. WHEN
THE SUN GOES DOWN.
THE STARS COME OUT."
-Unknown
WF

"DON'T YOU KNOW YET?
IT'S YOUR LIGHT THAT LIGHTS THE WORLD."
-Rumi
WF.

SOMETIMES THE BEST WAY TO APPRECIATE SOMETHING IS TO BE WITHOUT IT FOR A WHILE.
@wadeforbes

"A harvest of peace is
produced from a seed
of contentment."
—Proverb
WF, '20

WF. '20
"CREATIVITY IS INTELLIGENCE
HAVING FUN." -Albert Einstein

"MUSIC IS
THE SHORTHAND
OF EMOTION."
–Leo Tolstoy
WF, '20

CAN'T DANCE?
SPELL YOUR NAME
IN THE AIR WITH
YOUR BUM.
BOOM. NEXT
PROBLEM?
–Unknown
WF.'20

WF '20
"GIVING UP ON YOUR GOAL
BECAUSE OF ONE SETBACK
IS LIKE SLASHING YOUR
OTHER THREE TIRES
BECAUSE YOU GOT A FLAT."
–Unknown

"DO WHAT YOU LOVE AND YOU WILL NEVER HAVE A PROBLEM WITH ANOTHER MONDAY."
WF.20
-Anonymous

A dog may be
man's best friend..
But the horse
wrote history.
–Unknown
WF '20

"WHAT WOULD LIFE BE IF WE HAD NO COURAGE TO ATTEMPT ANYTHING?"
-Anonymous
WF.20

"IF YOU ARE MORE FORTUNATE
THAN OTHERS, BUILD A
LONGER TABLE.
NOT A TALLER FENCE."
-Anonymous
DAY 239
WF.20

"KINDNESS IS ALWAYS DIFFICULT TO GIVE AWAY BECAUSE IT KEEPS COMING BACK." –Anonymous

"TO APPRECIATE THE BEAUTY OF A SNOWFLAKE, IT IS NECESSARY TO STAND OUT IN THE COLD."
—Anonymous
WF,'20

"AN EMPTY
LANTERN
PROVIDES NO
LIGHT. SELF-
CARE IS THE
FUEL THAT
ALLOWS YOUR
LIGHT TO SHINE BRIGHTLY."
–Unknown
WF. '20

-Mark Twain
"WHENEVER YOU FIND YOURSELF ON THE SIDE OF THE MAJORITY, IT IS TIME TO PAUSE & REFLECT."

"A LIFE WITHOUT LOVE IS LIKE A YEAR WITHOUT SUMMER."
—Swedish Proverb
W.F.20

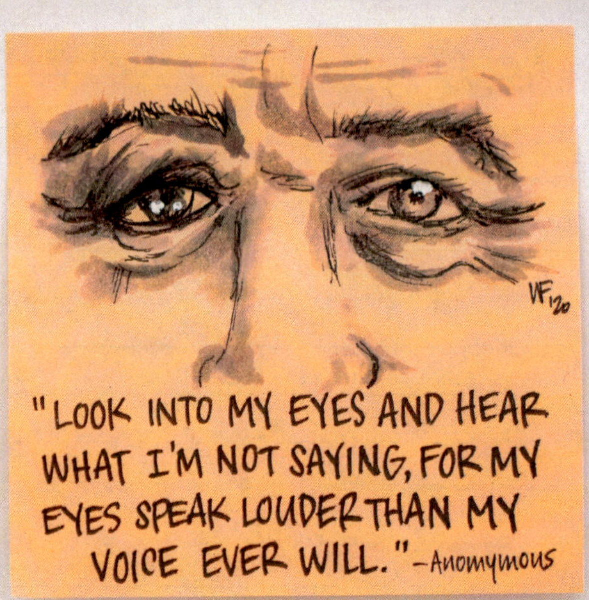
VF '20
"LOOK INTO MY EYES AND HEAR WHAT I'M NOT SAYING, FOR MY EYES SPEAK LOUDER THAN MY VOICE EVER WILL." –Anomymous

"HE/SHE WHO HAS A WHY TO LIVE FOR CAN BEAR ALMOST ANY HOW."
- Friedrich Nietzche
WF.20

"IF YOU IMPROVE BY 1% EVERY DAY, WITHIN A YEAR YOU'LL HAVE IMPROVED BY 365%."

—Anonymous

RELATIONSHIPS
LEARNING
EXERCISE
IMAGINATION
SERVICE
TALENTS
LOVE
RELAXING
COURAGE
EMPATHY

W.F. '20

WF 20
"NOT ALL STORMS COME TO DISRUPT YOUR LIFE. SOME COME TO CLEAR YOUR PATH."
—Anonymous

"AND STILL, AFTER ALL
THIS TIME, THE SUN
HAS NEVER SAID
TO THE EARTH,
"YOU OWE ME"
LOOK WHAT HAPPENS
WITH LOVE LIKE
THAT. IT LIGHTS
UP THE SKY."
-Rumi
WF.20

"THERE IS NO EXERCISE BETTER FOR THE HEART THAN REACHING DOWN AND LIFTING PEOPLE UP."
—John Holmes
WF. '20

"COURAGE DOESN'T MEAN YOU DON'T GET AFRAID. COURAGE MEANS YOU DON'T LET FEAR STOP YOU."
-Anonymous
FEAR
WF'20

"You can discover more about a person in an hour of play than in a year of conversation."
-Plato
WF'20

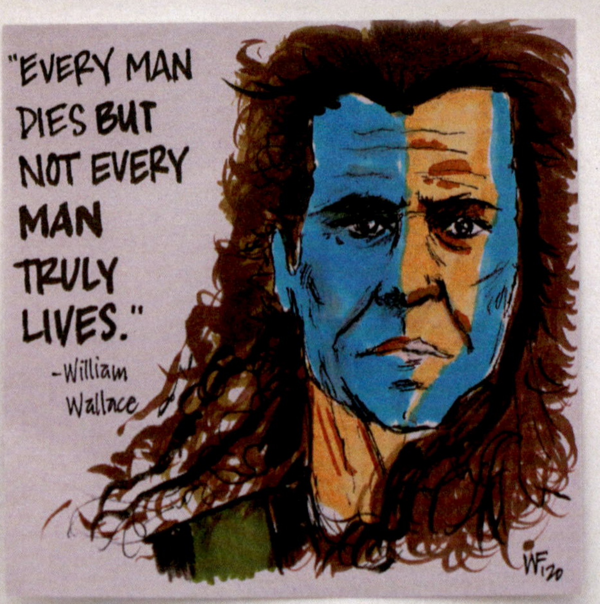
"EVERY MAN
DIES BUT
NOT EVERY
MAN
TRULY
LIVES."
-William
Wallace
WF '20

"SOMETIMES WHEN YOU ARE IN A DARK PLACE, YOU THINK YOU ARE BURIED, BUT ACTUALLY YOU'VE BEEN PLANTED."
-Anonymous
WF,'20

WF. '20
"Why should you feel anger at the world, as if the world would notice."
—Euripides

THE
TWO
MOST
POWERFUL
WARRIORS
ARE
PATIENCE
AND
TIME.
-Leo Tolstoy

TIBETAN PROVERB
WF.20
"The secret to living well and longer is:
eat half, walk double, laugh triple, and
love without measure."

"AND I STILL
ONWARD HASTE
TO MY LAST NIGHT;
TIME'S FATAL WINDS
DO EVER FORWARD
FLY; SO EVERY DAY
WE LIVE, A DAY WE
DIE."
—Thomas Campion
WF, '20

DAY 219
WF '20
"MY HEART IS AT EASE KNOWING THAT WHAT IS MEANT FOR ME WILL NEVER MISS ME, AND THAT WHAT MISSES ME WAS NEVER MEANT FOR ME." -Al Shafi'ee

DON'T EXPECT THE SAME RESULTS
FROM THE THINGS THAT LOOK ALIKE...
—African Proverb

TOMORROW IS PREGNANT AND NO ONE KNOWS WHAT SHE WILL GIVE BIRTH TO.
-African Proverb
VF.20

AS LONG AS THERE
IS SOMEONE IN
THE SKY TO PROTECT
ME, THERE IS NO
ONE ON EARTH
WHO CAN BREAK ME.
—Unknown
WF. 20

WE ARE ALL IN THE GUTTER...
BUT SOME OF US ARE LOOKING
AT THE STARS.
-Oscar Wilde
WF.'20

YOUR
IMAGINATION
IS YOUR
PREVIEW
TO LIFE'S
COMING
ATTRACTIONS.
-EINSTEIN

WF '20
"THE SOLE MEANING OF LIFE IS TO SERVE HUMANITY." -Leo Tolstoy

LOVE ALL, TRUST A FEW, DO WRONG TO NONE
-Shakespeare

FOR TOMORROW BELONGS TO THE PEOPLE WHO PREPARE FOR IT TODAY.
-African Proverb
WF.20

WEAR GRATITUDE LIKE A
CLOAK AND IT WILL FEED
EVERY CORNER OF YOUR LIFE.
-Rumi
WF. 20

HOWEVER LONG THE NIGHT,
THE DAWN WILL BREAK.
W.F. 20
-African Proverb

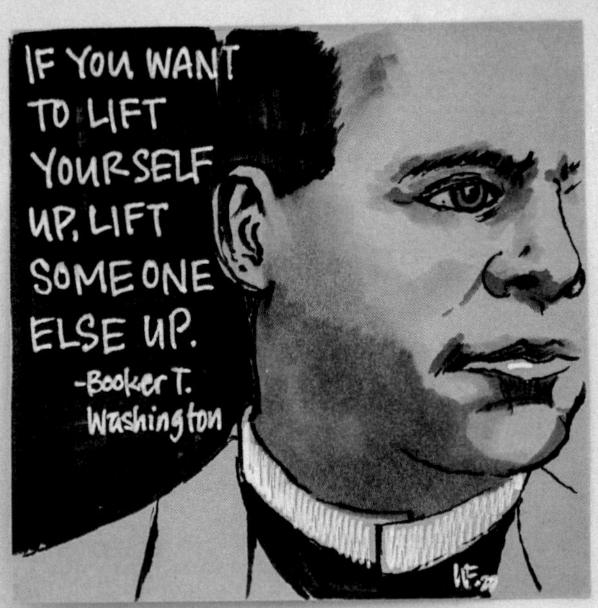
IF YOU WANT TO LIFT YOURSELF UP, LIFT SOMEONE ELSE UP.
-Booker T. Washington

LISTEN TO THE SILENCE.
IT HAS MUCH TO SAY.
- Rumi
WF. 20

"SHE WHO HAS PEACE OF
MIND DISTURBS NEITHER
HERSELF NOR ANOTHER."
-Epicurus
WF 20

"DO NOT GIVE UP,
THE BEGINNING IS ALWAYS
THE HARDEST."
WF '20

"A SNOWFLAKE IS ONE OF THE MOST FRAGILE CREATIONS, BUT LOOK WHAT THEY CAN DO WHEN THEY STICK TOGETHER."

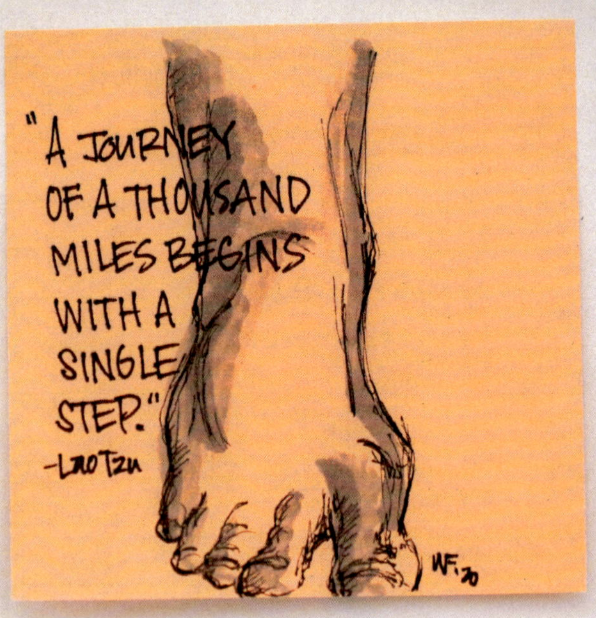
"A JOURNEY
OF A THOUSAND
MILES BEGINS
WITH A
SINGLE
STEP."
-LAO TZU
W.F. '20

"AN ELEPHANT
WHICH KILLS
A RAT IS NOT
A HERO."
-African
Proverb
WF '20

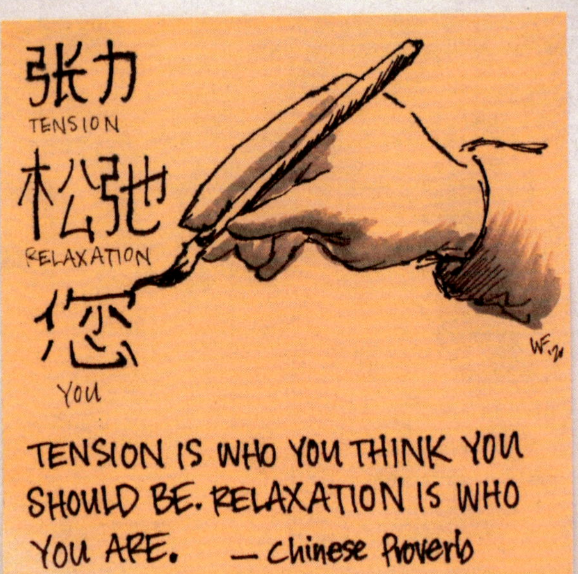
张力
TENSION
松弛
RELAXATION
您
YOU
TENSION IS WHO YOU THINK YOU SHOULD BE. RELAXATION IS WHO YOU ARE. — Chinese Proverb

"YOU CANNOT DO KINDNESS TOO SOON, FOR YOU NEVER KNOW HOW SOON IT WILL BE TOO LATE."

—Ralph Waldo Emerson

"The art of being
wise is the art of
knowing what to
OVERLOOK."
—William James

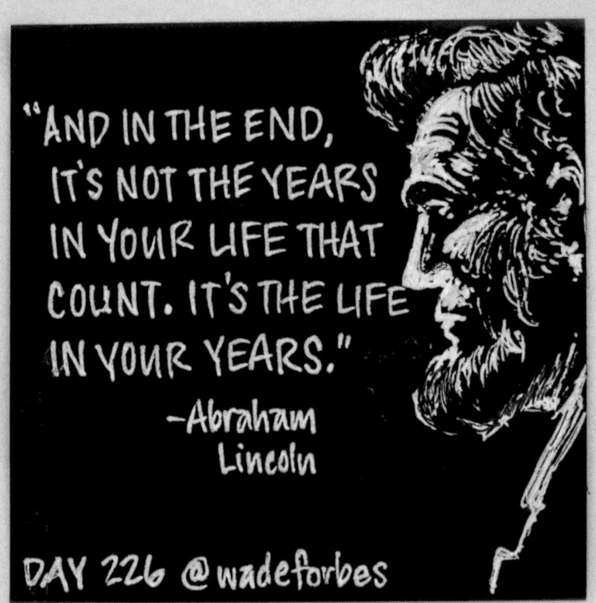
"AND IN THE END,
IT'S NOT THE YEARS
IN YOUR LIFE THAT
COUNT. IT'S THE LIFE
IN YOUR YEARS."
-Abraham
Lincoln
DAY 226 @wadeforbes

"EITHER WRITE SOMETHING WORTH READING OR DO SOMETHING WORTH WRITING."
—Benjamin Franklin
WF.'20

"COURAGE IS
RESISTANCE TO
FEAR, MASTERY
OF FEAR, NOT
ABSENCE OF FEAR."
-Mark
Twain

DON'T CONFUSE THE PEOPLE
WHO ARE ALWAYS AROUND
WITH THE ONES WHO
ARE ALWAYS THERE.
-Unknown

REMEMBER WHEN YOU SEE SOMEONE AT THE TOP OF THE MOUNTAIN, THEY DID NOT FALL THERE.
-Author Unknown

"EVERY BATTLE
IS WON BEFORE
IT IS EVER
FOUGHT."
–Sun Tzu

THE SECRET OF CHANGE IS TO FOCUS ALL OF YOUR ENERGY NOT ON FIGHTING THE OLD, BUT ON BUILDING THE NEW.
-Socrates
W.F. '20

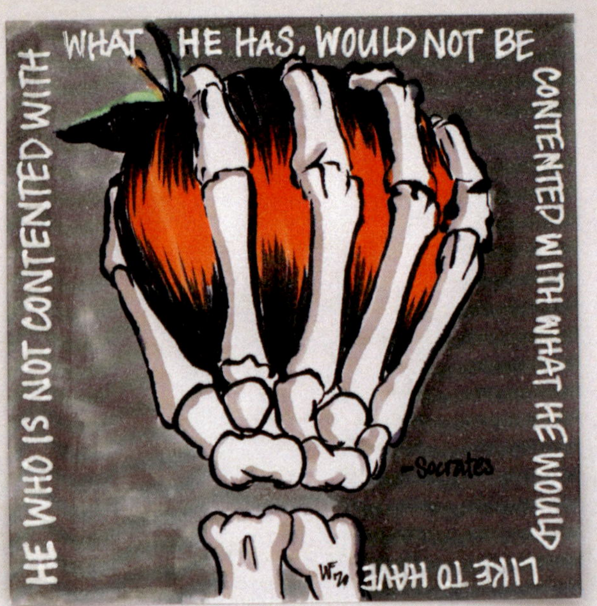
HE WHO IS NOT CONTENTED WITH WHAT HE HAS, WOULD NOT BE CONTENTED WITH WHAT HE WOULD LIKE TO HAVE
-Socrates

IT IS
BETTER
TO BE
WISE
ALONE,
THAN MAD
WITH THE
REST OF
THE WORLD.
-Unknown

MOST MEN LEAD LIVES OF QUIET DESPERATION AND GO TO THEIR GRAVES WITH THE SONG STILL IN THEM.
-Henry David Thoreau

WHEN LIFE CHANGES
TO BE HARDER
CHANGE
YOURSELF
TO BE
STRONGER.
-Unknown

YOU HAVE TO FIGHT THROUGH SOME BAD DAYS TO EARN THE BEST DAYS OF YOUR LIFE.
–Unknown

WE MUST WALK
CONSCIOUSLY
ONLY PART WAY
TOWARD OUR
GOAL,
AND THEN LEAP
IN THE DARK
TO OUR SUCCESS.
-Auther Unknown

WHY NOT GO OUT ON A LIMB?
THAT'S WHERE THE FRUIT IS.
- Mark Twain

Now That Your Journal Is Full...

If you enjoyed this book, would you be so kind as to take a moment, go to Amazon, and look up the title, "90 Days to Write Your Way to Spring: the Winter Journal," and leave a short review? Even if you only had time to go through a couple of pages you will be able to leave a review and, if you desire, go back later and add to it once you've had a chance to complete the book.

Your first impressions are very useful, so don't worry if you have only time now to review one or two elements.

Finally, note that books succeed by the kind, generous time readers take to leave honest reviews. This is how other readers learn about books that are most beneficial for them to buy. I thank you in advance for this very kind gesture of appreciation. It means the world to me.

Acknowledgements.

Any time we find ourselves having a positive impact, a successful interaction, or a feel-good moment, it is a moment to reflect on not what, but who got you there.

A huge thank you to my wife, Megan. Talk about choosing your partner wisely. Not only did I marry my best friend, but I also married the person who brings out the best version of me, and who helped bring the right words to this project. We started RedTale Communications LLC together to help people tell a better story and this dream came to life. It sounds cliché, but there is no way I could have done this without her.

Thank you to Owen and Ryan who insist that I am not allowed to critique my work. Not a day goes by where they do not tell me how much they love my drawings.

Thank you to my parents for always believing that my art was worth doing. I am still drawing things that go on their fridge.

My next round of thank you's goes out to: Maegin Graves and her awesome Dunkin' Donuts team (Loren, Dorian, Alec, Taylor, and Jon), Megan Scott for her tailored advice, "if you love what you are doing, then you must spread your light to the world.", Jon Bostock for asking me to illustrate "The Elephant's Dilemma" and customer reviews with Truman's. The confidence he and Alex Reed instilled in me early on in my illustration journey has catapulted me further than I could have imagined in a short amount of time.

Thank you to Rich Austin at Trembling Giant Marketing for the beautiful high res images, page layout, great talks, and for tolerating my amateur Christopher Walkin impressions at the beginning of each call we had together..

Thank you to my amazing book club and my supportive circle of friends, who remind me how easily spreading kindness brings about joy, and to my family for proving again and again that when you lead with love, it is the ultimate way to believe you are doing the right thing.

Last but not least, thank you to Julie Anixter for introducing me to Melissa Wilson, my publisher at Networlding. When I came to an obstacle in the road about what to do with these daily quotes, I reached out to Julie and boy did she deliver. If you have not formed a network yet, don't panic. People like Julie and Melissa are working their magic in the world. The hope and positivity being spread is more powerful than the fear and doubt.

To learn more about the author and stay connected to the quotes journals, please visit www.redtale.com